ROLE OF FAMILY AND COMMUNITY IN DISABILITY MANAGEMENT

NAKUL KHATRI

I would like to dedicate this book to my father, Mr. Devinder Singh. He always showed great faith in my abilities and pushed me to go beyond them.

Contents

Foreword

Dear Students,

I am delighted to introduce this book, specifically designed for those pursuing special education courses such as D.Ed and B.Ed. The book is strictly adhered to the latest RCI syllabus and has been curated in a lucid manner, mostly in the form of points. The language used in this book is easy to understand, making it accessible for students from various backgrounds.

Special education is a difficult topic that calls for a thorough knowledge of diverse disabilities, teaching approaches, and intervention techniques. This book has been written to provide you a thorough understanding of the subject matter by addressing a variety of special education-related subjects. You may easily understand difficult topics because of the way the content is organised, with a focus on real-world applications.

Finally, I am confident that this book will be a valuable resource for you as you pursue your special education studies. It is a must-read for anyone interested in pursuing a career in this field, and I am confident that it will be a valuable resource for many years to come. I wish you the best of luck in your studies and hope that this book will assist you in reaching your objectives.

Best wishes,

Nakul khatri

Syllabus

Unit 1: Understanding family

- Family; meaning, definition, and characteristics - Families in the Indian context;
- Structure, types of families, and its impact on children's development;
- Family culture and practices & its influence on children's mental and physical well-being;
- Parenting and its types and its impact on children's education;
- Challenges of parents of 21st-century modern-day learners;

Unit 2: Family and disability

- Stages of reaction and impact and coping of having a child with a disability;
- Involving parents in diagnosis, fitment of aids, and acceptance of disability by family;
- Importance of family involvement and advocacy in interventional practices;
- Concept, components, and strategies of family empowerment;
- Partnering for interventional practices;

Unit 3: Role of family in early childhood care and education (ECCE)

- Parents as first teachers and family as the first school;
- Role of family in developing and executing IFSP and IEPs;
- Family's role in developing foundational literacy in young children;
- Supporting learning at home, school, and in after-school activities;
- Role of family in facilitating inclusive education ;

Unit 4: Community for disability rehabilitation

- Concept and types of communities;
- Role of community in prevention early identification, and intervention of disability;
- Community-based inclusive development – need, importance, and

strategies;
- Creating enabling environments- mobilising local community resources towards the rehabilitation of persons with disabilities

- Issues and challenges in the rehabilitation of children with a disability in the community;

<u>Unit 5: Role of community in the education of children with disabilities</u>

- Community awareness about disabilities - early identification, intervention, and education
- Community support for home-based education in times of disasters;
- Collaboration with Aganwadis and other Governmental agencies for education of children with disabilities

- Community as a stakeholder in special and inclusive education;
- Safeguarding children with disabilities and their families in the communities;

Preface

The foundational unit of any community, the family, is crucial in determining how an individual's life will turn out. Understanding the significance of family and community in the rehabilitation of disabled children has become significant in today's society due to the growing obstacles faced by families.

This book's objective is to provide readers a thorough understanding of how families and communities play a crucial role in the education and rehabilitation of disabled children. The book is organized into five sections, each of which concentrates on a different facet of family and community involvement in the lives of children with disabilities.

We examine the idea of family, its types, structure, and impact on children's development in the first unit. We dig into the many parenting philosophies and the difficulties parents encounter when trying to raise today's learners.

The second unit focuses on coping mechanisms and stages of reaction for parents of disabled children. We also discuss the value of family advocacy and involvement in interventional practices.

The third lesson covers the significance of the family in the upbringing and education of young children. We look at the crucial function of parents as the child's first teachers and how they might encourage learning at home, at school, and in extracurricular activities.

The fourth section emphasizes the value of community involvement in the rehabilitation of people with disabilities. We investigate the various communities' functions in impeding early diagnosis and treatment of impairments. Also, we go over methods for fostering inclusive communities and utilizing available local resources for the rehabilitation of people with impairments.

The community's contribution to the education of children with disabilities is a topic we cover in the fifth unit. We investigate how well-informed the community is on disability and how supportive they are of education at home and in emergency situations. We also examine the community's involvement in special and inclusive education as well as its cooperation with governmental organizations for educational purposes.

In conclusion, everyone interested in the rehabilitation and education of children with impairments will find this book to be a useful resource.

It serves as a manual for assisting families, educators, and community members in building a welcoming and inclusive environment for children who are disabled.

I welcome suggestions and constructive feedback from my readers. You can message me at khatrinakul4@gmail.com.

Nakul khatri

March 06, 2023

Acknowledgements

To my wife Jyoti Baliyan, I would like to convey my sincere gratitude for her unfailing support and inspiration as I wrote this book. My continual source of inspiration has been her love and affection.

Vardaan Khatri and Antriksh Khatri, my two dearest boys, whose love and support have kept me inspired, also deserve my gratitude. I can't thank them enough for being here; it's been a joy and a comfort.

In addition, I want to thank Notion Press for making publishing easy for me by giving me access to their online resources and straightforward publishing procedure. Their crew has been tremendously helpful and productive in assisting me in finishing this book.

Finally, I want to thank all the readers who have helped me along the way to become a published author. Your suggestions and words of support have been quite helpful, and I appreciate them.

I want to use this opportunity to once again convey my sincere gratitude to my wife, my sons, Notion Press, and my readers for their unflagging support and inspiration.

I appreciate you everyone.

Sincerely,

Nakul khatri

Role of family and community
in
Disability management
By
Nakul Khatri
(M.sc physics, M.A psychology, M.A education, PGDGC)
Special education teacher Directorate of education Delhi

CHAPTER ONE

Understanding family

Introduction

A family is a social unit that consists of individuals who are related to each other by blood, marriage, or adoption. It is considered to be the basic unit of society, and its members share a strong bond that is built over time through shared experiences and traditions. The concept of family is universal and can be found in every culture and society throughout the world, although the specific form and structure of families may vary greatly.

The concept of family has evolved over time, and today, families come in many different shapes and sizes. Some families consist of a married couple with children, while others may include single parents, extended family members, or same-sex couples with children. Despite these differences, the common thread that ties all families together is the bond between its members, which is based on love, mutual support, and a shared sense of responsibility.

The family is a crucial source of support and stability in a person's life. It provides a sense of belonging, and its members can turn to one another for help and guidance in times of need. The family can also play a crucial role in a person's development, as it is often the first place where children learn about relationships, social norms, and cultural values. The experiences and interactions within the family can have a profound impact on a person's life and can shape their personality, beliefs, and behaviors.

One of the most important roles of the family is to provide a safe and secure environment for its members. This can take many forms, including providing a stable home life, financial support, and emotional support. The family can also help its members to develop a strong sense of self-esteem and self-worth, as well as provide a sense of belonging and connectedness.

In addition to providing support and stability, the family also plays a critical role in the transmission of cultural values and traditions. It is through the family that children learn about their heritage, cultural beliefs, and customs, and these experiences can shape their identity and beliefs for the rest of their lives. For many people, the family is also the source of their spiritual and religious beliefs, and it provides a sense of belonging and connection to a larger community.

The family can also be a source of conflict, as its members may have different opinions, beliefs, and values. However, it is through these conflicts that families can grow and strengthen their bonds, as they work together to resolve their differences and find common ground. In order for families to be successful, it is important for its members to have open and honest communication, and to respect each other's opinions and beliefs.

Despite the challenges that families may face, they remain an essential part of society. They provide a sense of security, stability, and support that is essential for a healthy and happy life. Whether through shared experiences, traditions or simply being there for one another, the family is a powerful force that shapes who we are and helps us to thrive.

The meaning of family can differ greatly depending on the individual, and it can change over time as a person's circumstances and relationships change. However, the fundamental idea of family as a group of individuals who are connected by blood, marriage, or adoption remains constant and it continues to play a critical role in our lives.

In conclusion, the family is a complex and dynamic unit that plays a vital role in our lives. It provides us with support, stability, and a sense of belonging, and it helps to shape who we are and our place in the world. Whether we are born into a family, create one of our own, or build relationships with those who become like family to us, the bond of family is one that lasts a lifetime.

Various definitions of family

Family is a concept that has been defined in many different ways, reflecting its complex and dynamic nature. Here are a few definitions of the family:

Biological definition: A family is defined as a group of individuals who are related to each other by blood or genetics. This definition focuses on the biological connections between family members.

1. **Legal definition:** Family is defined as a group of individuals who are recognized by law as being related. This definition often includes relationships established through marriage, adoption, or other legal

means.

2. **Sociological definition:** Family is defined as a group of individuals who share a close personal relationship and who live together or otherwise interact on a regular basis. This definition encompasses a wider range of relationships than the biological or legal definitions and includes families that are formed through choice, rather than by blood or law.

3. **Psychological definition:** Family is defined as a group of individuals who share a close personal relationship and who provide emotional support, security, and a sense of identity to one another. This definition emphasizes the emotional and psychological connections between family members.

4. **Anthropological definition:** Family is defined as a social group that includes people who are related by blood, marriage, or adoption, and who share common beliefs, values, and customs. This definition takes into account the cultural and social aspects of family life.

These are just a few of the many different definitions of family, and it is important to note that the meaning of family can differ greatly depending on the individual and the culture in which they live. However, regardless of the specific definition, the family remains a critical aspect of human life, providing support, stability, and a sense of belonging to its members.

There are several key themes that are common to many of the different definitions of family. Some of these include:

1. **Relationships:** Most definitions of family emphasize the importance of close personal relationships between family members. Whether these relationships are based on biology, law, or choice, they are characterized by strong emotional bonds and a sense of mutual support and responsibility.

2. **Shared experiences:** Family is often seen as a group of individuals who share common experiences, traditions, and cultural values. These shared experiences can help to strengthen the bond between family members and provide a sense of belonging and identity.

3. **Support:** Family is often described as a source of support for its members. This can take many forms, including emotional support, financial support, and practical assistance. Family members may turn to each other in times of need and can count on one another for help and guidance.

4. **Stability:** Family is seen as a source of stability in a person's life, providing a sense of security and stable home life. This stability can be especially important for children, who may look to their families for guidance and support as they grow and develop.
5. **Cultural and social ties:** Family is often seen as a cultural and social group, with its own traditions, beliefs, and values. These cultural and social ties can help to shape a person's identity and provide a sense of connection to a larger community.

While these themes are common to many definitions of family, it is important to remember that the specific form and structure of families can vary greatly. For example, families can be composed of married couples with children, single parents, extended family members, or same-sex couples with children.

Additionally, the role and importance of family can differ greatly depending on the culture and society in which it exists. For example, in some cultures, the family is considered to be the most important source of support and stability, while in others, the individual is emphasized.

Characteristics of family

There are several key characteristics that define a family, including:

1. **Relationships:** Family is defined by the close personal relationships between its members. These relationships can be based on biology, law, or choice, but they are characterized by strong emotional bonds and a sense of mutual support and responsibility.
2. **Shared experiences:** Family members share common experiences, traditions, and cultural values. These shared experiences can help to strengthen the bond between family members and provide a sense of belonging and identity.
3. **Support:** Family members are expected to provide support for one another, whether it be emotional, financial, or practical. Family members may turn to each other in times of need and can count on one another for help and guidance.
4. **Stability:** Family is seen as a source of stability in a person's life, providing a sense of security and stable home life. This stability can be especially important for children, who may look to their families for guidance and support as they grow and develop.

5. **Cultural and social ties:** Family is often seen as a cultural and social group, with its own traditions, beliefs, and values. These cultural and social ties can help to shape a person's identity and provide a sense of connection to a larger community.

6. **Communication:** Good communication is important in any family, as it helps family members to understand each other's perspectives and needs. Open and honest communication can also help to resolve conflicts and build stronger relationships.

7. **Flexibility:** Family dynamics can change over time, and families need to be flexible in order to adapt to these changes. For example, families may need to adjust their routines or expectations as children grow and develop, or as family members face new challenges or experiences.

8. **Love and affection:** Family is defined by the love and affection that exists between its members. Whether it be through hugs, kind words, or shared experiences, love, and affection are essential to the health and well-being of any family.

9. **Roles and responsibilities:** Family members often have specific roles and responsibilities within the family unit. For example, parents may be responsible for providing financial support and emotional care, while children may be responsible for household chores and school work.

10. **Values and beliefs:** Family members often share similar values and beliefs, which can help to shape their behavior and decisions. These shared values and beliefs can also help to bring family members together and provide a sense of unity and purpose.

11. **Tradition:** Family traditions and rituals can be an important part of family life, helping to create a sense of continuity and connection over time. These traditions can include things like holiday celebrations, family meals, or special events and activities.

12. **Diversity:** Despite their shared experiences and values, families can also be diverse in many ways, such as race, religion, ethnicity, and sexual orientation. Celebrating and embracing this diversity can help to create a stronger and more inclusive family unit.

13. **Conflict:** Conflicts are a normal part of family life, and they can arise due to a variety of reasons such as differences of opinion, misunderstandings, or changes in family dynamics. While conflicts can be difficult, they can also provide an opportunity for growth and understanding within the family.

14. **Resilience:** Families often face challenges and obstacles, but they are also capable of overcoming these difficulties and growing stronger as a result. This resilience can be fostered by the support and love of family members, as well as a shared sense of purpose and commitment.

Family in the Indian context

In India, family plays a central role in both personal and cultural life. Indian families are typically large, extended, and closely knit, with strong ties between parents, grandparents, children, and other relatives.

In the Indian context, family is seen as a source of support, security, and stability, with family members expected to provide for each other in times of need. Family is also seen as a source of identity and cultural connection, with families often sharing common traditions, beliefs, and values.

One unique aspect of Indian families is the emphasis on arranged marriages, which are still common in many parts of the country. In an arranged marriage, families play a key role in selecting a suitable spouse for their child. The process typically involves the families getting to know each other and discussing the potential match, with the goal of finding a compatible partner who shares similar values and cultural backgrounds.

The joint family system, where several generations of a family live together under one roof, is also common in India. This system can provide many benefits, including shared resources, support for elderly family members, and a sense of community and belonging.

Family values such as respect for elders, filial piety, and a strong work ethic are highly valued in India and are often passed down from generation to generation. Family honor and reputation are also considered important, with families often taking steps to protect their good name and reputation within their community.

In conclusion, family plays a crucial role in the lives of people in India, providing support, stability, and a sense of identity and cultural connection. The close-knit nature of Indian families, combined with traditional values and cultural practices, make family an integral part of Indian life and society.

Structure of families

The structure of a family can vary widely depending on cultural, social, and historical factors. However, there are several common family structures that are widely recognized. Here are a few examples:

A. Nuclear family

The nuclear family is the most common type of family structure and consists of a mother, a father, and their children. This type of family structure is often seen as the basic unit of society, with the parents providing both emotional and financial support for their children.

One of the key characteristics of a nuclear family is the close relationship between parents and children. Children in nuclear families receive individual attention from their parents and are encouraged to develop their own identities and interests. The parents provide a supportive and loving environment for their children and play a central role in their lives.

Another characteristic of the nuclear family is that the parents are typically responsible for the financial stability of the family. In many cases, the father works outside the home to provide for the family, while the mother may work outside the home or stay at home to care for the children. The division of labor in a nuclear family can vary, and many families today have both parents working outside the home.

Nuclear families can provide a number of benefits for their members. For example, children in nuclear families have a strong sense of security and stability, as they are able to rely on their parents for support and guidance. Additionally, the close relationship between parents and children in a nuclear family can provide children with a strong sense of identity and self-esteem.

However, nuclear families can also face a number of challenges. For example, the close relationship between parents and children can sometimes lead to increased pressure on the parents to provide emotional support and guidance. Additionally, the financial responsibilities of a nuclear family can be demanding, and parents may struggle to balance their work and family responsibilities.

Despite these challenges, the nuclear family remains the most common type of family structure and is valued for the close relationships and support it provides to its members. In many cases, the nuclear family is the foundation of a strong and supportive community, with parents and children working together to create a loving and supportive environment.

It is important to note that the structure of a nuclear family can vary depending on cultural, social, and historical factors. For example, in some cultures, multiple generations may live together as a nuclear family, while in others, nuclear families may be more isolated from extended family members. Additionally, the division of labor within a nuclear family can vary, with both parents working outside the home, one parent staying at home, or a combination of both.

In conclusion, the nuclear family is a common and important type of family structure that provides a close relationship between parents and children, as well as emotional and financial support for its members. While it can face challenges, the nuclear family remains an important source of support and stability for its members and is valued for the close relationships and support it provides.

A. Extended families

An extended family is a family structure that includes extended relatives in addition to the nuclear family, such as grandparents, aunts, uncles, and cousins. This type of family structure is common in many cultures and is often seen as a way to provide support, security, and a sense of belonging for its members.

One of the key characteristics of an extended family is the presence of multiple generations living together or in close proximity. This can provide a wealth of support and resources for both children and adults, with grandparents often playing a key role in the upbringing of grandchildren. The close relationships between extended family members can also provide a sense of stability and security, as well as a connection to family history and traditions.

Another important characteristic of extended families is the sharing of resources and responsibilities. For example, family members may share living spaces, financial resources, and responsibilities for caring for children and elderly relatives. This can help to lighten the burden on individual family members, especially those who may be struggling financially or with caring for children or elderly relatives.

In terms of the impact on children, growing up in an extended family can provide a wealth of positive experiences. Children may benefit from having multiple adults in their lives who provide love and support, as well as from exposure to different perspectives and experiences. Additionally, children may also benefit from the close relationships they form with their cousins and extended family members, which can provide a sense of connection and belonging.

However, living in an extended family can also have its challenges. For example, the close proximity of multiple family members can sometimes lead to conflicts or tensions, and it can be difficult to balance the needs and desires of multiple generations. Additionally, the sharing of resources and responsibilities can sometimes result in a lack of privacy or individual space.

Despite these challenges, extended families remain an important part of many cultures, providing a sense of belonging, support, and stability for their members. The close relationships and shared experiences of extended family members are a testament to the power and importance of family, and the role that extended families play in shaping the lives of their members.

It's worth noting that the structure of extended families can vary greatly depending on cultural, social, and historical factors. For example, in some cultures, extended families may live together in one household, while in others, they may live in separate homes but remain close in proximity and relationships.

In conclusion, the extended family is an integral part of many cultures, providing a sense of belonging, support, and stability for its members. The close relationships and shared experiences of extended family members are a testament to the power and importance of family, and the role that extended families play in shaping the lives of their members.

C. Single-parent families

A single-parent family is a family structure in which a single parent raises one or more children without the support of a partner. Single-parent families are becoming increasingly common in modern society and can result from a variety of circumstances, including divorce, the death of a partner, or the decision to raise a child as a single parent.

Despite the challenges that come with raising children as a single parent, many single-parent families are able to provide a loving and supportive environment for their children. Single parents often play multiple roles in their families, serving as both the primary caregiver and financial provider, which can result in increased stress and pressure. However, many single parents are able to rise to the challenge and provide a stable and loving home for their children.

In terms of the impact on children, growing up in a single-parent family can have both positive and negative effects. On one hand, children in single-parent families may benefit from a close relationship with their parents, as well as increased independence and self-reliance. On the other hand, they may also experience feelings of isolation, lack of a male or female role model, and financial insecurity.

It's important to note that single-parent families are diverse and can come in many different forms. For example, some single-parent families consist of a mother and her children, while others may consist of a father and his children. Additionally, some single-parent families may receive support from extended family members or other caregivers, while others may rely solely on the efforts of the single parent.

Despite the challenges that come with single parenthood, many single parents are able to provide a stable and loving environment for their children. With support from family, friends, and community resources, single-parent families can thrive and provide children with a foundation for a healthy and fulfilling life.

In conclusion, single-parent families are an important part of modern society, providing a loving and supportive environment for children despite the challenges of single parenthood. Despite the challenges that come with raising children as a single parent, many single-parent families are able to provide a stable and loving home for their children, and with the support of family, friends, and community resources, they can thrive and provide children with a foundation for a healthy and fulfilling life.

D. Blended families

A blended family, also known as a stepfamily, is a family structure that consists of a couple and their children from previous relationships. Blended families are becoming increasingly common in modern society, and can result from a variety of circumstances, including divorce, remarriage, and adoption.

Blended families can bring together a diverse group of individuals with different backgrounds, values, and experiences, which can lead to both challenges and benefits. On one hand, blended families can offer children the opportunity to expand their network of loved ones and form close relationships with new family members. On the other hand, blended families can also experience conflicts and tension as individuals work to establish new family dynamics and adjust to one another.

It's important for blended families to work together to establish a positive and supportive environment for all family members. This can involve setting clear boundaries and establishing a shared understanding of the roles and responsibilities of each family member. In some cases, blended families may also benefit from outside support, such as therapy or support groups, to help manage any challenges that arise.

In terms of the impact on children, growing up in a blended family can have both positive and negative effects. On one hand, children in blended families may benefit from a larger support network, as well as increased exposure to a variety of experiences and perspectives. On the other hand, they may also experience feelings of loss, confusion, and insecurity, particularly if the family structure changes frequently.

Despite the challenges that come with blending families, many blended families are able to thrive and provide a stable and loving environment for their children. With open communication, clear boundaries, and a commitment to working together, blended families can build strong and supportive relationships that benefit all family members.

In conclusion, blended families are an important part of modern society, offering children the opportunity to form close relationships with new family members and expand their support network. Despite the challenges that come with blending families, many blended families are able to thrive and provide a stable and loving environment for their children, and with open communication, clear boundaries, and a commitment to working together, they can build strong and supportive relationships that benefit all family members.

E. Same-sex parent families

Same-sex parent families are families in which one or both parents are of the same gender. Same-sex parent families can result from a variety of circumstances, including adoption, surrogacy, and biological conception through assisted reproductive technology

Same-sex parent families face unique challenges, including social stigma and discrimination, as well as a lack of legal recognition in some areas. Despite these challenges, many same-sex parent families are able to provide a stable and loving environment for their children.

In terms of the impact on children, research has consistently shown that children raised by same-sex parents fare just as well as children raised by different-sex parents in terms of their physical, psychological, and emotional well-being. Children raised by same-sex parents have the same opportunities for healthy development and successful outcomes as those raised by different-sex parents, including strong family relationships, academic achievement, and overall happiness.

It's important to note that same-sex parent families are diverse and can come in many different forms. For example, some same-sex parent families consist of two mothers, while others may consist of two fathers. Additionally, some same-sex parent families may include children from previous relationships, while others may be raising children together for the first time.

Despite the challenges that come with being a same-sex parent, many same-sex parent families are able to provide a stable and loving environment for their children, and with support from family, friends, and community resources, they can thrive and provide children with a foundation for a healthy and fulfilling life.

In conclusion, same-sex parent families are an important part of modern society, offering children the opportunity to grow up in a loving and supportive environment, regardless of the gender of their parents. Despite the challenges that come with being a same-sex parent, many same-sex parent families are able to provide a stable and loving home for their children, and with support from family, friends, and community resources, they can thrive and provide children with a foundation for a healthy and fulfilling life.

F. Grandparent-led families

Grandparent-led families refer to families in which grandparents take on the primary caregiving role for their grandchildren. This can occur for a variety of reasons, including the death of a parent, the incarceration of a parent, substance abuse, or other factors that prevent parents from providing care for their children.

Grandparent-led families can bring a unique set of challenges, as grandparents may face physical and emotional exhaustion from taking on a caregiving role later in life, as well as financial stress from supporting multiple generations. Additionally, grandparents may also face legal and practical barriers to obtaining custody or guardianship of their grandchildren.

Despite these challenges, many grandparents rise to the occasion and provide a stable and loving home for their grandchildren. In many cases, grandparent-led families provide a sense of stability and continuity for children, allowing them to maintain relationships with their families and communities and reducing the likelihood that they will enter the foster care system.

In terms of the impact on children, growing up in a grandparent-led family can have both positive and negative effects. On one hand, children in grandparent-led families may benefit from a sense of stability, security, and continuity, as well as close relationships with their grandparents. On the other hand, they may also experience feelings of loss and insecurity, particularly if they are separated from their parents or other family members.

It's important for grandparent-led families to receive support from community resources, such as legal services, financial assistance, and support groups, to help manage the challenges that come with taking on a caregiving role later in life. Additionally, community and government support can help ensure that grandparent-led families have access to the resources and support they need to provide a stable and loving environment for their grandchildren.

In conclusion, grandparent-led families are an important part of modern society, offering children the opportunity to grow up in a stable and loving environment, even in the absence of their parents. Despite the challenges that come with being a grandparent-led family, many grandparent-led families are able to provide a supportive and loving home for their grandchildren, and with support from community resources, they can thrive and provide children with a foundation for a healthy and fulfilling life.

Here's a table that summarizes the characteristics of different types of families:

Type of Family
Characteristics

Nuclear Family

Consists of a married couple and their children. The family is typically centered around the parents and their offspring.

Extended Family

Including grandparents, aunts, uncles, and cousins. The family often shares resources and provides emotional and practical support to one another.

Single-Parent Family

A family consisting of a single parent and their children. The parent is responsible for the upbringing and care of the children.

Blended Family

A family is composed of individuals who have come together through marriage or remarriage and brought with them children from previous relationships.

Same-Sex Parent Family

A family consisting of two parents of the same sex, who are raising children together.

Adoptive Family

A family consisting of individuals who have legally adopted a child or children.

Foster Family

Families in which individuals provide temporary care for children who have been removed from their biological families due to abuse, neglect, or other circumstances.

Please note that this table is not exhaustive and there may be other types of families that are not listed here. Additionally, families can exhibit characteristics from multiple categories, so it's possible for a family to have elements of both a nuclear and extended family

Structure of families

Families can take on many different structures and forms. Some common family structures include:

- Nuclear family: A family unit consisting of a married couple and their children.
- Extended family: A family unit that includes relatives beyond the immediate family, such as grandparents, aunts, uncles, and cousins.
- Single-parent family: A family unit consisting of a single parent and their children.
- Blended family: A family unit created when two people with children from previous relationships come together and form a new family.
- Same-sex parent family: A family unit consisting of two parents of the same sex and their children.
- Adoptive family: A family unit consisting of individuals who have legally adopted a child or children.

- Foster family: A family unit consisting of individuals who provide temporary care for children who have been removed from their biological families.
- Joint family: A family unit in which two or more married couples and their children live together in the same household.

It's important to note that families can take on many different structures and forms, and that these structures can change over time. Additionally, families can be composed of individuals who are related by blood, marriage, adoption, or other means, and can consist of a wide variety of cultural, ethnic, and socioeconomic backgrounds.

Role of family type in child development

The role of different types of families in child development can vary, but some generalizations can be made. Here are the roles of different types of families in child development:

1. Nuclear family: In a nuclear family, the parents typically play a central role in a child's development. They provide the child with a stable home environment, care, and support, and are typically the primary source of emotional and financial support.
2. Extended family: In an extended family, the child may have access to multiple adults who can offer love, support, and guidance. Grandparents, aunts, uncles, and cousins can provide the child with additional role models and a sense of family history and tradition.
3. Single-parent family: In a single-parent family, the parent plays a central role in the child's development and may

Family culture and practices

Family culture refers to the shared beliefs, values, behaviors, customs, and traditions that define a family and shape its functioning. Family culture is created and transmitted through various means, including family rituals and routines, stories and legends, religious and spiritual beliefs, and educational practices. Family culture can also be shaped by factors such as the family's social and economic status, cultural background, and geographic location.

Family practices refer to the specific behaviors and activities that families engage in to fulfill their roles and functions. These practices can include things such as mealtime routines, holiday celebrations, religious practices, and educational activities. Family practices also often reflect the family's culture and values and serve as a way to reinforce and transmit these cultural elements from one generation to the next.

Both family culture and practices play a significant role in child development. The family culture provides a child with a sense of identity and a framework for understanding the world, while the family practices provide structure and stability to the child's daily life. Family culture and practices can also shape a child's beliefs, values, and behaviors, and have a lasting impact on their social and emotional development.

It's important to note that family culture and practices can change over time and may vary across different families. Additionally, families can have multiple cultures and practices that coexist within the same family unit.

Parenting

Parenting refers to the process of raising and nurturing a child or children. It encompasses a wide range of activities and responsibilities, including providing for physical and emotional needs, promoting social and intellectual development, and helping children to become independent. Parenting is one of the most important and challenging aspects of human life, and it can have a profound impact on children's health, well-being, and future success.

There are many different styles of parenting, each with its own strengths and weaknesses. Some common styles of parenting include authoritarian, permissive, and authoritative parenting. Authoritarian parenting is characterized by strict rules and high expectations, while permissive parenting is characterized by a lack of rules and discipline. Authoritative parenting is a balanced approach that involves setting high expectations while also providing support and nurturing.

Parenting can be both rewarding and challenging, and it requires a significant investment of time, energy, and patience. Effective parenting requires a good understanding of child development, a commitment to promoting children's well-being, and a willingness to adapt to the changing needs of children as they grow and develop.

Despite its challenges, parenting can also bring great joy and fulfillment. It provides an opportunity to build close relationships with children and to shape their lives in meaningful and positive ways. With patience, dedication, and a commitment to lifelong learning, parents can play a crucial role in helping their children to reach their full potential.

Parenting can be defined in a few different ways:

- **Raising and nurturing a child:** Parenting involves providing for the physical, emotional, and social needs of a child, helping them to grow and develop, and guiding them toward independence.
- **The act of being a parent:** Parenting is the role that one takes on when one becomes a parent, which includes the responsibilities and duties associated with raising a child.
- **A set of practices and beliefs:** Parenting can also refer to the specific beliefs, values, and practices that a parent brings to their role in raising a child. This can include beliefs about discipline, education, and other aspects of child-rearing.
- **An ongoing process:** Parenting is an ongoing process that begins at birth and continues throughout a child's life. It involves adapting to the changing needs of children as they grow and develop, and continually adjusting one's parenting practices to meet these needs.

In all of these definitions, the common thread is that parenting is the process of raising and nurturing a child, and it involves a wide range of responsibilities and practices. Regardless of the specific approach or style of parenting that one adopts, the ultimate goal is to provide children with the support and guidance they need to reach their full potential.

There are several different types of parenting styles, each of which has its own unique characteristics and impact on children's development. The following are some of the most commonly recognized parenting styles:

1. **Authoritarian parenting:** Authoritarian parenting is characterized by strict rules, high expectations, and a focus on obedience and respect for authority. Parents who use this style of parenting set clear expectations and enforce them with firm discipline, often using punishment to correct misbehavior. Children raised by authoritarian parents may struggle with independence and self-expression, but they may also have a strong sense of responsibility and discipline.
2. **Permissive parenting:** Permissive parenting is characterized by a lack of rules and discipline and a focus on meeting children's desires and needs. Parents who use this style of parenting are often warm and nurturing, but they may also have difficulty setting boundaries and enforcing consequences for misbehavior. Children raised by permissive parents may have difficulty with self-discipline and responsibility, but they may also be more confident and self-expressive.

3. **Authoritative parenting:** Authoritative parenting is characterized by high expectations and a supportive and nurturing environment. Parents who use this style of parenting set clear expectations, but also provide support and guidance to help children meet these expectations. Children raised by authoritative parents are typically independent and self-confident, with high levels of academic and social success.

4. **Uninvolved parenting:** Uninvolved parenting is characterized by a lack of involvement and a disregard for children's needs and feelings. Parents who use this style of parenting may be neglectful or absent, and they may not provide adequate support or attention to their children. Children raised by uninvolved parents may struggle with low self-esteem, social isolation, and a lack of emotional support.

In addition to the four main types of parenting styles described above, there are a few other parenting styles that have been identified and studied:

1. **Indulgent parenting:** Indulgent parenting, also known as permissive-indulgent parenting, is characterized by high levels of warmth and nurturing, but a lack of structure and rules. Parents who use this style of parenting often allow their children to make decisions for themselves and may not set clear boundaries or consequences for misbehavior. Children raised by indulgent parents may have difficulty with self-regulation and discipline, but they may also be highly creative and self-expressive.

2. **Neglectful parenting:** Neglectful parenting, also known as uninvolved-neglectful parenting, is characterized by a lack of warmth, attention, and support. Parents who use this style of parenting may be emotionally distant or unavailable, and they may not provide adequate care for their children. Children raised by neglectful parents may experience neglect, abuse, or abandonment, and they may struggle with a wide range of social, emotional, and behavioral problems.

3. **Helicopter parenting:** Helicopter parenting, also known as overprotective parenting, is characterized by high levels of control and involvement in a child's life. Parents who use this style of parenting may be overly involved in their children's activities, decisions, and friendships and they may have difficulty letting go and allowing their children to make decisions on their own. Children raised by helicopter parents may struggle with independence and self-reliance, but they may

also have high levels of emotional security and support.

4. **Free-range parenting:** Free-range parenting is characterized by a focus on independence and self-reliance. Parents who use this style of parenting may give their children the freedom to explore, take risks, and make decisions on their own, with the goal of fostering independence and resilience. Children raised by free-range parents may be highly confident and self-sufficient, but they may also be vulnerable to dangers or risks that they are not prepared to handle.

Each of these parenting styles can have positive and negative impacts on children's development, and it's important for parents to find a balance that works for them and their children. The most effective parenting style is one that is responsive to the changing needs of the child and the family, and that takes into account the unique strengths and weaknesses of each parent and child.

Characteristics of a good parenting style

A good parenting style is one that is supportive, nurturing, and responsive to the individual needs and development of the child. Here are some of the key characteristics of a good parenting style:

1. **Warmth and affection:** Good parenting involves showing warmth, affection, and love towards children, creating a supportive and nurturing environment.
2. **Clear boundaries and expectations:** Good parenting involves setting clear boundaries and expectations for children, while also being flexible and responsive to their changing needs and development.
3. **Consistency:** Good parenting involves being consistent and predictable in providing love, support, and discipline.
4. **Active involvement:** Good parenting involves being actively involved in children's lives, paying attention to their experiences, feelings, and needs, and providing guidance and support as needed.
5. **Communication:** Good parenting involves good communication with children, listening to their perspectives, and encouraging open and honest dialogue.
6. **Empathy:** Good parenting involves showing empathy and understanding towards children, recognizing their experiences and feelings, and providing comfort and support when needed.

7. **Positive reinforcement:** Good parenting involves using positive reinforcement to encourage good behavior, rather than relying solely on punishment or negative consequences.
8. **Encouragement of independence:** Good parenting involves encouraging children to develop independence and self-reliance, while also providing support and guidance as needed.
9. **Respect for individuality:** Good parenting involves respecting children's unique needs, personalities, and interests, and supporting their individual development and growth.
10. **Flexibility:** Good parenting involves being flexible and adaptive, and recognizing that the needs and characteristics of children change as they grow and develop.

Good parenting also involves promoting the physical, emotional, social, and intellectual well-being of children. Here are some additional ways in which good parenting can positively impact children:

1. **Physical health:** Good parenting involves promoting physical health by providing nutritious food, encouraging physical activity, and supporting regular doctor visits and vaccinations.
2. **Emotional health:** Good parenting involves promoting emotional health by providing a supportive and nurturing environment, recognizing and responding to children's emotions, and teaching them healthy coping skills.
3. **Social skills:** Good parenting involves promoting social skills by encouraging positive relationships with peers, modeling positive social interactions, and teaching children how to navigate social situations.
4. **Cognitive development:** Good parenting involves promoting cognitive development by exposing children to new experiences, providing educational opportunities, and encouraging exploration and learning.
5. **Moral and ethical development:** Good parenting involves promoting moral and ethical development by setting a good example, teaching values and beliefs, and encouraging children to make responsible and ethical decisions.
6. **Self-esteem and self-worth:** Good parenting involves promoting self-esteem and self-worth by recognizing and acknowledging children's strengths, encouraging their independence, and providing positive reinforcement.

7. **Resilience:** Good parenting involves promoting resilience by teaching children coping skills, encouraging independence, and providing support and guidance during difficult times.

8. **Strong relationships:** Good parenting involves promoting strong relationships by providing emotional support, modeling positive communication, and encouraging open and honest dialogue.

The 21st century has brought many new challenges for parents of children who are learning and growing in a rapidly changing world. **Some of the major challenges faced by parents today include:**

1. **Technology:** With the increasing use of technology and social media, parents must navigate the complex and ever-changing world of online communication and content. This can include issues such as cyberbullying, which involves using technology to harass, threaten, or harm others, as well as exposure to inappropriate or harmful content. Parents must also be aware of the potential impact of technology on children's attention spans and social skills, as overuse of technology can lead to decreased face-to-face communication and increased screen time. To address these challenges, parents can set clear boundaries and rules around technology use, educate themselves about online safety, and encourage alternative forms of play and communication.

2. **Work-life balance:** Many parents today face the challenge of balancing work and family responsibilities, and finding ways to effectively manage their time and energy. This can lead to feelings of guilt, stress, and burnout, and can have a negative impact on family relationships and well-being. To address this challenge, parents can prioritize self-care, communicate openly with their partners and family members, and work to find flexible work arrangements that allow them to be present and involved in their children's lives.

3. **Changing educational expectations:** The 21st century has brought new and rapidly changing expectations for education, and parents must work to stay informed and involved in their children's academic progress. This can include adapting to new educational technologies, navigating changes in curriculum and assessment practices, and ensuring that their children have access to high-quality educational resources and opportunities. To address these challenges, parents can stay informed about changes in education, be actively involved in their children's

education, and work with teachers and administrators to advocate for their children's needs and interests.

4. **Mental health and well-being:** Mental health and well-being are becoming increasingly important topics, and parents must be attuned to the emotional and mental health needs of their children, and be prepared to seek help and support when needed. This can include addressing issues such as anxiety, depression, and behavioral problems, and promoting healthy coping skills and resilience. To address these challenges, parents can educate themselves about mental health and well-being, communicate openly with their children about their feelings and experiences, and seek support from mental health professionals and community resources when needed.

5. **Diversity and inclusion:** As society becomes more diverse and inclusive, parents must work to promote and support diversity and inclusivity in their homes and communities. This can include teaching children about different cultures and experiences, encouraging empathy and understanding, and working to address biases and prejudice. To address these challenges, parents can seek out diverse books, media, and educational resources, engage in cross-cultural exchange and learning and model positive and inclusive behavior in their own lives.

6. **Financial stability:** Many parents today face financial challenges and uncertainty, and must work to provide for their families while also ensuring that their children have access to the resources and opportunities they need for success. This can include navigating the cost of education, balancing work and family responsibilities, and managing household finances. To address these challenges, parents can seek out financial resources and support, communicate openly and honestly with their partners and children about money, and work to promote financial literacy and stability in their homes and communities.

7. **Busy schedules:** With the many demands of work, school, extracurricular activities, and other commitments, families can often feel overwhelmed and overscheduled. This can lead to increased stress, burnout, and decreased quality time spent together as a family. To address this challenge, parents can prioritize self-care; create opportunities for unstructured play and relaxation, and work to maintain a healthy work-life balance.

CHAPTER TWO

Family and disability

Having a disabled child is a life-changing experience for parents. It can cause a wide range of emotions and challenges that can be difficult to deal with. The stage of reaction, impact, and coping with a disabled child is a model that helps to understand the emotional and psychological reactions that parents experience when they learn that their child has a disability. The model also suggests coping strategies that can assist parents in adjusting to their new reality.

Stages of reaction of having a child with a disability

1. **Shock and denial:** When most parents learn that their child has a disability, their first reaction is shock and denial. They may be numb and unable to believe what they are hearing. They may also experience disbelief and believe that an error has occurred. During this stage, parents may avoid discussing the disability and struggle to accept that their child has a lifelong condition.

2. **Grief and mourning:** The following stage is marked by grief and mourning. Parents may experience feelings of loss for the life they had planned for their child. They may be saddened by the loss of the child they hoped to have and the future they had planned. They may also experience sadness, guilt, and a sense of helplessness. This stage can be especially difficult for parents as they try to accept the reality of their child's disability.

3. **Guilt and self-blame:** Guardians could also feel guilty and blame themselves. They may believe that they are to blame for their child's disability or they might have done something different to prevent it. These emotions can be overwhelming and can contribute to depression and anxiety.

4. **Anger and resentment:** As parents adjust to their child's disability, they may feel emotions of anger and resentment. They may be angry with the world or with themselves for their predicament. They may also be resentful of people who don't face similar difficulties.

5. **Acceptance and adjustment:** Parents can begin to adjust to their new reality once they accept their child's disability. They may start looking for information and resources to assist their child and family. They may also begin to envision a new future for their child and seek novel approaches for promoting their child's development.

6. **Advocacy and empowerment:** Once parents accept their child's disability, they may feel empowered and motivated to advocate for their child's needs. They might look for support groups or organizations that can offer them resources and information. They may also become more involved in their child's care and education, working to ensure that their child receives the best services possible.

7. **Resilience and hope:** Resilience and hope characterize the model's final stage. Parents who have gone through the stages of reaction, impact, and coping with a disabled child are often incredibly resilient. They've learned to adapt to their situation's challenges and developed coping strategies to help them manage their emotions and support their child's development. They also have hope for their child's future and are dedicated to giving their child the best life possible.

Impact and adjustment to having a disabled child

For families, having a child with a disability can have a big, lasting impact. A variety of feelings and behaviors, including shock, grief, guilt, wrath, and anxiety, may be experienced by parents. The effects can also be felt by siblings, who may feel left out or resentful of the focus on the disabled child. It's possible that the entire family will need to get used to new routines, therapies, doctor appointments, and financial demands.

Coping strategies can assist families in dealing with the effects of having a disabled child. Seeking support from family and friends, joining support groups or online communities, seeking professional counseling or therapy, and engaging in self-care activities such as exercise or hobbies are all common coping strategies. Families may also benefit from education and training about their child's specific disability, as well as advocacy and service access resources.

Coping usually involves multiple phases, which include surprise, rejection, negotiating, frustration, depressed mood, and approval. These stages are not necessarily sequential and may occur concurrently or in a different order for different people. A parent, for example, may experience shock and denial at the time of diagnosis, followed by anger and bargaining as they grapple with the implications of their child's disability. They may eventually reach a point of acceptance with support and coping strategies.

It's important to remember that coping with a child's disability is a lifelong process, with ups and downs along the way. Furthermore, depending on the severity and type of disability, as well as other factors such as cultural background and socioeconomic status, the impact and coping strategies may differ. As a result, it is critical to tailor coping strategies to the specific needs and circumstances of each family.

Understanding the impact and coping strategies for families of children with disabilities is important for several reasons.

Firstly, it helps to raise awareness and reduce the stigma around disabilities. By recognizing the challenges and experiences of families, society can become more supportive and inclusive towards individuals with disabilities and their families.

Secondly, understanding the impact and coping strategies can help professionals provide better support and services to families. Healthcare providers, therapists, educators, and social workers can use this knowledge to offer appropriate information, referrals, and resources to families.

Thirdly, understanding the impact and coping strategies can help families themselves. It can help them feel less alone and more validated in their experiences. It can also provide guidance on where to seek support and how to manage the impact of having a child with a disability.

Involving parents in the diagnosis, fitment of aids, and acceptance of disability by the family is an important aspect of supporting children with disabilities. Here's a detailed explanation of each:

Involving parents in diagnosis: When a child is diagnosed with a disability, it can be a challenging time for the family. Involving parents in the diagnosis process can help them understand the condition and the best course of action to support their child. Healthcare providers should provide clear information about the diagnosis, prognosis, and available interventions. They should also encourage parents to ask questions and voice their concerns. Involving parents in the diagnosis process can help them feel more in control and empowered to take action.

Fitment of aids: Assistive technology and devices can make a significant difference in the lives of children with disabilities. These devices can include mobility aids, communication aids, hearing aids, and vision aids. Involving parents in the fitment of these aids is crucial to ensure that they are appropriate for their child's needs and that they are used effectively. Healthcare providers should work with parents to assess their child's needs, determine the best type of assistive technology, and provide training on how to use it. Parents should be encouraged to ask questions and provide feedback on the effectiveness of the aids.

Acceptance of disability by the family: Acceptance of disability by the family is an ongoing process that can be challenging for some families. Involving parents in the acceptance process can help them understand the impact of the disability on their child and family and develop coping strategies. Healthcare providers should provide education and support to families to help them understand their child's strengths and challenges and to promote a positive attitude towards the disability. Families should be encouraged to seek out support groups or counseling to help them manage their emotions and build resilience.

Importance of family involvement and advocacy in interventional practices

Family involvement and advocacy in interventional practices are essential for promoting positive outcomes for children with disabilities. Here's a detailed explanation of the importance of family involvement and advocacy in interventional practices:

1. **Improves outcomes:** Family involvement and advocacy are key factors in ensuring the success of interventional practices for children with disabilities. When families are actively involved in the intervention process, they are more likely to understand their child's needs, communicate effectively with professionals, and implement interventions at home. This can lead to better outcomes, including improved behavior, social skills, communication, and academic performance.

2. **Builds trust and rapport:** Family involvement in interventional practices helps build trust and rapport between families and professionals. When families feel included in the decision-making process and have access to information and resources, they are more likely to trust and respect the professionals working with their children. This can lead to a more

collaborative approach, with families and professionals working together to support the child's needs.

3. **Provides a holistic approach:** Family involvement and advocacy in interventional practices provide a holistic approach to supporting children with disabilities. Families can provide valuable insights into their child's strengths, challenges, and preferences, which can help professionals develop more effective interventions. Families can also provide support and resources at home, which can complement the interventions provided by professionals.

4. **Empowers families:** Family involvement and advocacy in interventional practices can help empower families to take an active role in their child's care. When families are included in the decision-making process and have access to information and resources, they can feel more confident in their ability to support their child's needs. This can lead to increased self-efficacy and resilience, which can benefit both the child and the family.

5. **Advocates for the child:** Family advocacy is an important component of family involvement in interventional practices. When families advocate for their child's needs, they can help ensure that their child receives the appropriate services and support. Family advocacy can also help promote inclusive practices and policies, which can benefit not only the child but also other children with disabilities.

In conclusion, family involvement and advocacy in interventional practices are essential for promoting positive outcomes for children with disabilities. When families are included in the decision-making process and have access to information and resources, they can provide valuable insights and support that can complement the interventions provided by professionals. Family involvement and advocacy can also help build trust and rapport, provide a holistic approach, empower families, and advocate for the child's needs.

Concept of family empowerment

The concept of family empowerment refers to the process of strengthening the capacities, resources, and decision-making abilities of families to promote their well-being and achieve their goals. Family empowerment is based on the belief that families are the primary agents of change and can play a vital role in improving their own lives and the lives of their communities.

Empowering families involves providing them with the knowledge, skills, and support they need to make informed decisions and take actions that will improve their quality of life. It also involves acknowledging and respecting the unique strengths, values, and experiences of each family.

Family empowerment can take many different forms, depending on the specific needs and circumstances of each family. Some common strategies for empowering families include:

1. **Providing education and training:** Families may need support to develop skills and knowledge in areas such as parenting, health, financial management, and job skills. Education and training programs can help families acquire these skills and build their confidence and self-efficacy.

2. **Enhancing social support:** Families may benefit from having access to peer support groups, community networks, and other sources of social support. Social support can help families cope with challenges, reduce isolation, and build social capital.

3. **Advocating for families:** Family empowerment can involve advocating for policies and programs that support families and promote their well-being. Advocacy efforts can include lobbying for changes in laws and policies, building alliances with other organizations, and raising public awareness about issues affecting families.

4. **Encouraging participation in decision-making:** Empowering families involves encouraging their active participation in decision-making processes that affect their lives. This can include involving families in the planning and implementation of programs and services, soliciting their feedback and input, and promoting their representation in decision-making bodies.

5. **Providing resources and access to services:** Empowering families may involve providing them with access to resources such as affordable housing, healthcare, childcare, and transportation. It may also involve connecting families with community-based services and programs that can support their specific needs.

Components of family empowerment
The following are some of the key components of family empowerment:

1. **Information and Education:** The first component of family empowerment is providing families with access to information and

education. Families need to understand the issues that affect them and how they can take action to improve their situation. This includes information on health, education, financial management, parenting, and other topics relevant to their needs.

2. **Skill-building:** The second component of family empowerment is skill-building. Families need to develop the skills necessary to take action and achieve their goals. This includes communication skills, problem-solving skills, leadership skills, and other skills that are relevant to their needs.

3. **Support and Networking:** The third component of family empowerment is providing families with support and networking opportunities. Families need to feel supported and connected to others who share their concerns and experiences. This includes access to peer support groups, community networks, and other sources of social support.

4. **Advocacy and Representation:** The fourth component of family empowerment is advocating for the rights and interests of families. Families need to have a voice in decision-making processes that affect them. This includes advocating for policies and programs that support families and promoting their representation in decision-making bodies.

5. **Access to Resources:** The fifth component of family empowerment is providing families with access to resources. Families need access to affordable housing, healthcare, childcare, and other resources that support their well-being. This includes connecting families with community-based services and programs that can support their specific needs.

6. **Strengthening Family Relationships:** The sixth component of family empowerment is strengthening family relationships. Families need to have positive and healthy relationships with each other in order to effectively navigate challenges and achieve their goals. This includes promoting effective communication, conflict resolution, and other relationship-building skills.

7. **Cultural Sensitivity:** The seventh component of family empowerment is being culturally sensitive to the diverse needs of families. Families come from diverse cultural backgrounds and have unique experiences and values. It is important to understand and respect these differences in order to effectively support and empower families.

Strategies for family empowerment

There are several strategies that can be used to empower families, including:

1. **Education and Training:** Education and training programs can help families develop the knowledge and skills they need to make informed decisions and take action. These programs may include parenting classes, financial management workshops, job skills training, and other forms of education that are relevant to the needs of the family.
2. **Peer Support Groups:** Peer support groups provide families with the opportunity to connect with others who share their experiences and concerns. These groups may be facilitated by trained professionals or may be led by peers who have lived experience with similar challenges.
3. **Advocacy and Policy Change:** Advocacy efforts can help families to influence policy and promote changes that benefit them. Advocacy may include lobbying for changes in laws and policies, building alliances with other organizations, and raising public awareness about issues affecting families.
4. **Case Management and Navigation:** Case management and navigation services can help families to access the resources and services that they need. Case managers can assist families in identifying their needs and connecting them with appropriate services in the community.
5. **Strengthening Family Relationships:** Building strong and healthy family relationships is essential to family empowerment. This may involve promoting effective communication, conflict resolution, and other relationship-building skills.
6. **Community-Based Programs and Services:** Community-based programs and services can provide families with access to resources and support that are tailored to their needs. These programs may include healthcare services, childcare programs, after-school programs, and other services that support families.
7. **Leadership Development:** Developing leadership skills can help families to become more active in their communities and promote positive change. Leadership development programs may include training in advocacy, public speaking, and other skills that are relevant to community leadership.

Partnering for interventional practices

Partnering for interventional practices involves collaborating with families, professionals, and community organizations to provide effective support and services to individuals and families. The partnership is essential for successful interventional practices because it ensures that all stakeholders are involved in the process and that services are tailored to the needs of each individual and family. The following are some of the key principles of partnering for interventional practices:

1. **Family-Centered Care:** Partnering for interventional practices should be family-centered. This means that families should be involved in decision-making and planning and that services should be tailored to meet their needs and preferences.
2. **Collaborative Decision-Making:** Partnership involves collaborative decision-making, where all stakeholders have a voice in the process. This helps to ensure that services are effective and that families are satisfied with the outcomes.
3. **Culturally Responsive:** Partnering for interventional practices should be culturally responsive. This means that services should be respectful of the diverse cultural backgrounds and experiences of families and that services should be tailored to meet their unique needs.
4. **Evidence-Based Practices:** Partnering for interventional practices should be based on evidence-based practices that have been shown to be effective in supporting individuals and families. This helps to ensure that services are effective and that families are receiving the best possible support.
5. **Continuous Quality Improvement:** Partnership involves continuous quality improvement, where services are continually evaluated and improved based on feedback from families and stakeholders. This helps to ensure that services are effective and that families are satisfied with the outcomes.
6. **Professional Development:** Partnering for interventional practices involves ongoing professional development for all stakeholders involved. This ensures that professionals are up-to-date on the latest research and best practices and that they have the skills and knowledge needed to effectively support families.
7. **Community Partnerships:** Partnering for interventional practices involves building partnerships with community organizations to provide comprehensive support and services to families. This helps to ensure

that families have access to a wide range of resources and support and that services are coordinated and effective.

Advantages of Partnering for interventional practices

Partnering for interventional practices has many advantages for families, professionals, and community organizations. Some of the key advantages of partnering for interventional practices include:

1. **Improved outcomes for families:** Partnering with interventional practices can improve outcomes for families by providing them with more comprehensive support and services that are tailored to their unique needs. By working together, families, professionals, and community organizations can develop a more coordinated approach to supporting families, which can lead to better outcomes for children and families.

2. **Increased access to resources:** Partnering for interventional practices can increase access to resources for families. By working with community organizations, families can access a wider range of resources and services, including healthcare, childcare, and other social services. This can help to address the multiple needs of families and provide them with the support they need to thrive.

3. **More effective use of resources:** Partnering for interventional practices can lead to more effective use of resources. By collaborating and coordinating services, professionals, and organizations can avoid duplication of services and ensure that resources are being used in the most effective way possible.

4. **Enhanced communication and collaboration:** Partnering for interventional practices can enhance communication and collaboration among professionals and organizations. This can improve the quality of care and services provided to families, and ensure that families receive more comprehensive and coordinated support.

5. **Increased professional development opportunities:** Partnering for interventional practices can provide professionals with increased opportunities for professional development. By working with other professionals and organizations, professionals can learn about new approaches and best practices, and can develop new skills and knowledge.

6. **Stronger communities:** Partnering for interventional practices can lead to stronger communities. By working together, families, professionals, and community organizations can build stronger relationships, promote positive change, and create more supportive and connected communities.

Overall, partnering for interventional practices can have many advantages for families, professionals, and community organizations. By working together, we can provide more comprehensive, coordinated, and effective support to families, and help to build stronger, more supportive communities.

CHAPTER THREE

Role of family in early childhood care and education (ECCE)

Parents: The first teachers

Parents are the first and most important teachers for children. From birth, children are learning and develop at a rapid pace, and parents play a crucial role in shaping their children's development. Research has shown that children whose parents are actively involved in their learning and development tend to have better outcomes in school and in life.

The concept of parents as first teachers is based on the idea that parents are in the best position to support their children's learning and development. Parents know their children better than anyone else, and they have a unique understanding of their children's strengths, interests, and learning styles. By working with their children from an early age, parents can help to lay the foundation for their children's future success.

There are many ways in which parents can act as their children's first teachers. Some of the key strategies include:

1. **Talking and Listening:** From the moment they are born, children are listening and learn from the world around them. Parents can support their children's language development by talking to them, reading to them, and listening to them. This can help to build children's vocabulary, comprehension, and communication skills.

2. **Play and Exploration:** Play is essential for children's learning and development. Parents can support their children's play and exploration by providing them with a safe and stimulating environment, and by

engaging in play with them. This can help to foster children's creativity, imagination, and problem-solving skills.

3. **Modeling:** Parents are powerful role models for their children. By modeling positive behaviors and attitudes, parents can help to shape their children's values and beliefs. This can include modeling kindness, empathy, and respect, as well as modeling a love of learning and a growth mindset.

4. **Providing Structure and Routine:** Children thrive on structure and routine. By providing consistent routines and expectations, parents can help to support their children's learning and development. This can include setting regular meals and bedtimes, establishing a daily routine, and creating a learning environment that is organized and predictable.

5. **Encouraging Independence:** As children grow and develop, they naturally become more independent. Parents can support their children's independence by providing them with opportunities to make choices, take risks, and learn from their mistakes. This can help to build children's confidence, resilience, and problem-solving skills.

6. **Advocating for Their Children:** Parents are their children's best advocates. By staying informed about their children's education and development, and by advocating for their children's needs and interests, parents can help to ensure that their children receive the best possible support and services.

The benefits of parents as first teachers are many. Research has shown that children whose parents are actively involved in their learning and development tend to have better academic outcomes, as well as better social and emotional outcomes. By working with their children from an early age, parents can help to lay the foundation for their children's future success.

In addition to supporting their children's learning and development, parents as first teachers can also have a positive impact on families and communities. When parents are actively involved in their children's education and development, they are more likely to be engaged in their communities and to be advocates for positive change. This can help to build stronger, more connected communities that are supportive of children and families.

There are many programs and initiatives that support the concept of parents as first teachers. These include home visiting programs, early childhood education programs, and parent education and support programs. These programs can provide parents with the tools and resources they need to support their children's learning and development, as well as connect them with other parents and community resources.

In conclusion, parents are the first and most important teachers for children. By supporting their children's learning and development from an early age, parents can help to lay the foundation for their children's future success.

Family: The first school

The family is often referred to as the first school for children. This is because children learn many important skills and values from their families that will shape their development and future success. The family is the first social institution that children encounter and plays a crucial role in preparing them for life outside the home.

There are many ways in which the family can act as the first school for children. Some of the key areas of learning include:

1. **Language Development:** Children learn language by listening to and interacting with others. The family is the first place where children are exposed to language, and it plays a crucial role in developing their language skills. By talking to their children, reading to them, and engaging in conversation, parents can support their children's language development from an early age.

2. **Socialization:** Socialization is the process by which children learn the social norms, values, and behaviors of their culture. The family is the first place where children learn about socialization, as they observe and imitate the behaviors of their parents and siblings. By modeling positive social behaviors and providing opportunities for social interaction, parents can help to shape their children's socialization.

3. **Emotional Development:** The family also plays a critical role in children's emotional development. By providing a safe and nurturing environment, parents can help children to develop emotional regulation, empathy, and a sense of self-worth. This can include providing consistent routines and boundaries, as well as offering emotional support and validation.

4. **Academic Skills:** While the family is not typically thought of as a place for formal education, it can play a role in preparing children for academic success. By reading to their children, providing educational toys and games, and supporting homework and school projects, parents can help

to build their children's academic skills and readiness for school.

5. **Life Skills:** Finally, the family can also help to prepare children for the practical skills they will need in life. This can include teaching them how to cook, clean, and manage money, as well as providing guidance on navigating social and cultural norms.

The benefits of the family as the first school are many. Children who receive a strong foundation from their families are more likely to have better academic, social, and emotional outcomes. They are also more likely to have stronger relationships with their families and to be better prepared for life outside the home.

In addition to supporting children's development, the family as the first school can also have a positive impact on families and communities. When families are strong and supportive, they can help to build stronger communities and support positive social change.

There are many resources and programs available to support families in their role as the first school. These include parenting education and support programs, home visiting programs, and early childhood education programs. By connecting families with these resources and offering support and guidance, communities can help to ensure that all children have access to the benefits of the family as the first school.

In conclusion, the family is often referred to as the first school for children. By supporting children's language development, socialization, emotional development, academic skills, and life skills, families play a critical role in preparing children for success in life. The family as the first school can have a positive impact on children, families, and communities, and there are many resources and programs available to support families in this important role.

Role of family in developing and executing IFSP and IEPs

Individualized Family Service Plans (IFSPs) and Individualized Education Plans (IEPs) are important tools for children with special needs to receive the support they need to succeed in school and life. The development and execution of these plans require the active participation of families to ensure that the child's unique needs and strengths are recognized and addressed. Here, we will discuss the role of the family in developing and executing IFSPs and IEPs.

1. **Developing the Plan:**

The first step in developing an IFSP or IEP is to gather information about the child's strengths, needs, and interests. This information is typically gathered through assessments, observations, and interviews with the child, family members, and professionals who work with the child. The family plays a crucial role in this process by providing information about their child's development, behaviors, and preferences. This information helps to ensure that the plan is personalized and responsive to the child's individual needs.

1. **Setting Goals and Objectives:**

Once the information has been gathered, the next step is to set goals and objectives for the child. These goals and objectives should be specific, measurable, and based on the child's strengths and needs. The family plays a crucial role in this process by providing input on the goals and objectives that are important for their child. The family's perspective is essential in ensuring that the plan is realistic and achievable.

3. **Identifying Services and Supports:**

The next step is to identify the services and supports that the child will need to achieve the goals and objectives set out in the plan. These services and supports may include therapy, specialized instruction, assistive technology, and other accommodations. The family plays a crucial role in this process by providing input on the services and supports that have been helpful for their child in the past and by advocating for services and supports that they believe will be beneficial for their child's success.

4. **Implementation of the Plan:**

The final step is to implement the plan. This involves putting the services and supports in place and monitoring progress toward the goals and objectives. The family plays a crucial role in this process by working with the professionals who are supporting their child to ensure that the plan is being implemented effectively. The family can provide feedback on how the plan is working, advocate for changes if needed, and ensure that their child is receiving the services and supports that they need.

In summary, the family plays a critical role in developing and executing IFSPs and IEPs for children with special needs. By providing information about their child's strengths, needs, and preferences, setting goals and objectives, identifying services and supports, and monitoring progress towards the goals and objectives, families can ensure that their child's needs are being addressed and that they are receiving the support they need to succeed in school and life. By working together with professionals, families can advocate for their children and ensure that they are receiving the services and support they need to reach their full potential.

Family's role in developing foundational literacy in young children

The development of foundational literacy skills is crucial for young children to become successful readers and writers later in life. Parents and families play a vital role in supporting the development of these skills. Here are some ways in which families can support the development of foundational literacy in young children:

1. **Creating a Language-Rich Environment:** Children need to be exposed to language to develop strong literacy skills. Families can create a language-rich environment by talking, singing, and reading to their children. By engaging in conversations with their children, families can model language use and help children develop their vocabulary and comprehension skills.

2. **Reading Aloud:** Reading aloud to children is one of the most effective ways to support the development of foundational literacy skills. Families can read books with their children, pointing out letters, sounds, and words. By reading to their children, families can also help build comprehension skills and expose children to different types of texts.

3. **Playing with Letters and Sounds:** Families can help children develop phonological awareness skills by playing games that focus on sounds, such as rhyming games or "I Spy" games that focus on initial sounds. Families can also help children learn the alphabet by singing the alphabet song or playing with letter magnets or blocks.

4. **Writing Activities:** Families can help children develop their writing skills by providing opportunities for them to practice writing, such as drawing pictures and labeling them with words, writing letters to family members or friends, or making shopping lists. By encouraging children to write, families can help them develop fine motor skills and gain confidence in their ability to write.

5. **Using Technology:** Families can use technology to support the development of foundational literacy skills by using educational apps or websites that focus on phonics, reading, and writing. Families can also use technology to access e-books, which can be a great way to expose children to different types of texts and develop their comprehension skills.

In conclusion, families play a critical role in supporting the development of foundational literacy skills in young children. By creating a language-rich environment, reading aloud, playing with letters and sounds, providing writing activities, and using technology, families can help their children develop the skills they need to become successful readers and writers later in life. It is essential for families to be involved in their child's literacy development, as it sets the foundation for their academic success and overall well-being.

Supporting learning at home, school, and in after-school activities

Supporting learning at home, school, and in after-school activities is crucial for children's academic success and overall well-being. Here are some ways families can support learning across these settings:

A. **At Home:** Families can support learning at home by creating a quiet and comfortable study space for their children, establishing a consistent homework routine, and providing the necessary supplies and resources to complete homework and assignments. Families can also help children develop good study habits by encouraging them to set goals, manage their time effectively, and stay organized.

B. **At School:** Families can support learning at school by building positive relationships with their child's teachers and school staff, attending parent-teacher conferences and school events, and volunteering in the classroom or school activities. By being involved in their child's education, families can communicate their child's needs and strengths to teachers, stay informed about their child's progress, and provide additional support and resources if needed.

C. **After-School Activities:** After-school activities can provide opportunities for children to explore their interests and develop new skills. Families can support learning in after-school activities by choosing activities that align with their child's interests and strengths, encouraging their child to participate in extracurricular activities, and providing transportation and necessary supplies. Families can also help their children set goals and track their progress in these activities.

In conclusion, supporting learning at home, school, and in after-school activities is essential for children's academic success and overall well-being. By creating a supportive and encouraging learning environment, families can help their children develop the skills they need to succeed in school and in life. It is important for families to be involved in their child's education and to work collaboratively with teachers and school staff to ensure that their child receives the necessary support and resources to reach their full potential.

Role of family in facilitating inclusive education

Inclusive education is a process of ensuring that all students, regardless of their abilities, backgrounds, or characteristics, have equal access to quality education. Families play a critical role in facilitating inclusive education for their children. Here are some ways in which families can support inclusive education:

1. **Advocacy:** Families can advocate for their child's right to inclusive education by working collaboratively with school staff and administrators to develop and implement individualized education plans (IEPs) or individualized family service plans (IFSPs). Families can also advocate for policy changes and resources to support inclusive education.

2. **Building Positive Relationships:** Families can build positive relationships with school staff and administrators to promote an inclusive school culture. By establishing open communication and trust, families can work collaboratively with school staff to identify and address their child's individual needs.

3. **Understanding Diversity and Inclusion:** Families can support inclusive education by learning about and valuing diversity and inclusion. This includes understanding their own biases and promoting a culture of respect and acceptance for all students, regardless of their abilities, backgrounds, or characteristics.

4. **Providing Support:** Families can provide support to their children and school staff by sharing their knowledge and expertise about their child's needs and strengths. This includes providing resources, such as assistive technology or specialized services, to support their child's learning and

participation in the classroom.

5. **Encouraging Participation:** Families can encourage their child's participation in school activities and events to promote a sense of belonging and social connectedness. By encouraging their child to participate in extracurricular activities and events, families can help their child develop social skills and relationships with peers.

6. **Fostering Independence:** Families can support inclusive education by fostering their child's independence and self-advocacy skills. This includes encouraging their child to make decisions, take responsibility for their learning, and communicate their needs and preferences to school staff and peers.

7. **Continuous Learning:** Families can continuously learn about and promote inclusive education by participating in workshops, training sessions, and support groups. This allows families to stay informed about new developments and best practices in inclusive education and to connect with other families and professionals.

In conclusion, families play a critical role in facilitating inclusive education for their children. By advocating for their child's right to inclusive education, building positive relationships with school staff and administrators, understanding diversity and inclusion, providing support, encouraging participation, fostering independence, and continuously learning, families can help create an inclusive and supportive school environment for all students. It is important for families to be involved in their child's education and to work collaboratively with school staff and administrators to ensure that their child receives the necessary support and resources to reach their full potential.

CHAPTER FOUR

Community for disability rehabilitation

Concept of communities

Communities are groups of individuals who come together based on shared interests, values, beliefs, or geographic locations. These groups can be as small as a neighborhood or as large as a nation. Communities can be formal or informal, and they can be physical or virtual.

1. **Physical communities** are groups of people who live in the same geographic location, such as a neighborhood or a city. These communities are often based on shared interests, values, and beliefs, as well as the physical environment in which they live. For example, a community of surfers might be based in a coastal town, while a community of artists might be based in a city with a thriving arts scene. Physical communities can provide individuals with a sense of belonging, social support, and a shared sense of identity.

2. **Virtual communities** are groups of people who come together online, based on shared interests, values, or beliefs. These communities can take many forms, such as social media groups, forums, or online gaming communities. Virtual communities allow individuals to connect with others who share their interests, regardless of their physical location. This can be especially valuable for people who live in remote areas or who have niche interests that are not well-represented in their physical communities.

Communities can also be formal or informal. **Formal communities** are those that have defined structures and institutions, such as governments, schools, or religious organizations. These communities often have clear rules and hierarchies, and they provide a sense of stability and order. **Informal communities,** on the other hand, are based on more fluid and informal relationships, such as friendships or shared interests. These communities can be less structured, but they can also be more flexible and adaptable to change.

One of the most important aspects of communities is the social support they provide. Social support refers to the assistance and encouragement that people give to each other, both emotionally and practically. This can include everything from listening to someone who is going through a difficult time, to providing financial or material assistance. Social support is important for maintaining mental and physical health, and it can help people to cope with stress and adversity.

Communities also play an important role in shaping individual and collective identities. Our identity is made up of a complex set of factors, including our gender, race, ethnicity, religion, and cultural background. These factors can be influenced by the communities in which we participate. For example, a person who grows up in a community that values academic achievement and hard work may be more likely to prioritize these values in their own life. Communities can also help individuals to develop a sense of belonging and connection to others who share their identity.

One of the challenges of communities is balancing the needs and interests of the group with those of the individual. Communities can provide individuals with a sense of belonging and social support, but they can also exert pressure on individuals to conform to group norms and expectations. This can lead to conflicts between individual and group needs, and it can create tension within communities.

Another challenge of communities is ensuring that they are inclusive and equitable. Communities can sometimes be exclusive, either intentionally or unintentionally, and this can lead to discrimination and marginalization of certain groups. It is important for communities to actively work to address these issues and create environments that are welcoming and supportive of all members.

In conclusion, communities are an important part of our social and cultural fabric. They provide us with a sense of belonging, social support, and identity, and they shape our values and beliefs. However, communities also present challenges, such as balancing the needs of the group with those of the individual, and ensuring that they are inclusive and equitable. By understanding these dynamics, we can work to create communities that are supportive, inclusive, and sustainable for all members.

Role of community in prevention early identification, and intervention of disability

Communities play a critical role in the prevention, early identification, and intervention of disabilities. Disability is a broad term that encompasses a range of physical, sensory, intellectual, and mental health impairments that can have significant impact on an individual's daily life. The World Health Organization estimates that around 15% of the world's population lives with a disability, making it a significant public health concern.

Prevention of disability involves reducing risk factors that can lead to disability in the first place. Community-based prevention programs can help to address some of the social, economic, and environmental factors that contribute to disability. These programs can include health promotion and disease prevention activities, such as immunizations and screenings, as well as interventions that target specific risk factors, such as smoking cessation programs, substance abuse prevention, and healthy lifestyle interventions. Communities can also work to improve access to education and employment opportunities, which can help to reduce poverty and improve social inclusion, both of which are important factors in preventing disability.

Early identification of disability is also crucial for effective intervention. Early detection and diagnosis of disabilities can lead to more timely and effective interventions, which can help to prevent or minimize the impact of the disability on an individual's daily life. Community-based screening programs can play an important role in identifying disabilities at an early stage. These programs can include developmental screening for children, hearing and vision screenings, and mental health screenings for adults.

Communities can also help to ensure that individuals with disabilities receive appropriate interventions and support. This can include access to medical care, rehabilitation services, assistive technology, and other resources that can help individuals to maximize their independence and quality of life. Community-based interventions can include providing home-based care services, facilitating social support networks, and promoting inclusive education and employment opportunities.

In addition, communities can work to address some of the social and environmental barriers that individuals with disabilities often face. This can include promoting accessible infrastructure and transportation, advocating for policies that promote inclusion and equal rights, and raising awareness about disability issues. Communities can also provide training and education to service providers and other community members to help them better understand and support individuals with disabilities.

In summary, communities play a crucial role in the prevention, early identification, and intervention of disabilities. By working to address risk factors, promoting early identification, and providing appropriate interventions and support, communities can help to improve the lives of individuals with disabilities and promote greater social inclusion and equity for all members of the community.

Need

Community-based inclusive development (CBID) is an approach to development that seeks to promote the inclusion of all members of a community, including those who are often marginalized or excluded, such as persons with disabilities, women, children, and the elderly. CBID aims to empower these individuals by ensuring their full participation in all aspects of community life, including decision-making processes, social, economic, and cultural activities, and access to essential services and infrastructure.

The need for CBID arises from the fact that many individuals and communities are excluded from mainstream development programs due to various social, economic, and cultural factors. This exclusion can be due to a variety of reasons, such as lack of access to education, discrimination, poverty, and social stigma. This exclusion often results in limited opportunities for participation in decision-making, reduced access to essential services, and limited economic opportunities. As a result, these marginalized individuals and communities are often left behind, leading to increased poverty, social inequality, and reduced economic growth.

CBID seeks to address these issues by working with communities to identify and address the specific needs of all members, including those who are marginalized or excluded. This approach recognizes that development is not just about economic growth but also includes social, cultural, and environmental factors. By empowering individuals and communities, CBID can promote greater social inclusion, reduce poverty, and improve overall quality of life.

CBID has several key benefits. First, it promotes the participation of all members of the community in decision-making processes, which can lead to more inclusive and equitable development outcomes. Second, CBID can improve access to essential services such as healthcare, education, and infrastructure, which are critical for economic growth and social development. Third, CBID can reduce social stigma and discrimination, promoting greater social cohesion and reducing conflict. Finally, CBID can help to build community resilience, by ensuring that all members are empowered to respond to challenges and adapt to changing circumstances.

However, CBID also faces several challenges. One major challenge is the lack of resources and infrastructure in many communities, particularly in rural and remote areas. Another challenge is the need for greater awareness and understanding of disability and other marginalized groups, which can lead to resistance or apathy from some community members. Finally, CBID requires strong collaboration between government, civil society organizations, and the private sector, which can be difficult to achieve in some contexts.

In conclusion, CBID is an important approach to development that seeks to promote greater social inclusion, reduce poverty, and improve overall quality of life for all members of a community. By addressing the specific needs of marginalized and excluded groups, CBID can help to build more resilient and inclusive communities, contributing to sustainable development and economic growth. However, the success of CBID depends on strong collaboration and commitment from all stakeholders, including government, civil society organizations, and the private sector.

Importance

CBID recognizes that development is not just about economic growth, but also includes social, cultural, and environmental factors. Here are some reasons why CBID is important:

1. **Promotes social inclusion:** CBID promotes the inclusion of all members of a community, including those who are often marginalized or excluded. By promoting the full participation of all members in community life, CBID can help to reduce social exclusion, discrimination, and stigma, and promote greater social cohesion and harmony.
2. **Empowers marginalized groups:** CBID aims to empower marginalized groups by ensuring their full participation in decision-making processes, social, economic, and cultural activities, and access to essential services and infrastructure. This can help to promote greater social and economic equality, reduce poverty, and improve overall quality of life for marginalized groups.
3. **Enhances economic growth:** CBID recognizes that development is not just about economic growth, but it can also contribute to economic

growth. By promoting greater social inclusion and reducing poverty, CBID can help to promote economic growth by creating more opportunities for participation in economic activities, reducing social inequality, and promoting greater access to education, healthcare, and other essential services.

4. **Builds community resilience:** CBID can help to build community resilience by ensuring that all members are empowered to respond to challenges and adapt to changing circumstances. By promoting greater social inclusion, reducing poverty, and promoting access to essential services, CBID can help to build more resilient and inclusive communities, contributing to sustainable development and economic growth.

5. **Addresses human rights:** CBID promotes the full enjoyment of human rights for all members of a community, including those who are often marginalized or excluded. By ensuring that all members of a community are able to participate fully in community life, CBID can help to promote greater respect for human rights and reduce discrimination and social exclusion.

Strategies

Here are some strategies for implementing CBID:

1. **Participatory approach:** CBID should be implemented using a participatory approach that involves all members of the community, including those who are often marginalized or excluded. This approach ensures that all members have a voice in the development process and that their needs are taken into account.

2. **Capacity building:** CBID should include capacity building activities that aim to empower marginalized groups, such as persons with disabilities, women, and youth. Capacity building can include training and education programs that help individuals develop skills and knowledge that will enable them to participate fully in community life.

3. **Accessible infrastructure:** CBID should ensure that community infrastructure is accessible to all members of the community, including persons with disabilities. This can include making public spaces, buildings, and transportation accessible, as well as providing accessible information and communication technologies.

4. **Advocacy and awareness-raising:** CBID should include advocacy and awareness-raising activities that aim to reduce discrimination and stigma towards marginalized groups, such as persons with disabilities. Advocacy can involve working with government officials, community leaders, and other stakeholders to promote the rights of marginalized groups, while awareness-raising can involve community education and outreach programs.

5. **Inclusive policies and programs:** CBID should promote the development of inclusive policies and programs that aim to reduce poverty, promote economic growth, and enhance social inclusion. This can include policies and programs that promote access to education, healthcare, and other essential services, as well as programs that promote economic development and job creation.

6. **Collaboration and partnerships:** CBID requires strong collaboration and partnerships between government, civil society organizations, and the private sector. Collaboration can involve working with government officials and other stakeholders to develop inclusive policies and programs, while partnerships can involve working with local businesses and other organizations to promote economic development and job creation.

In conclusion, CBID requires a range of strategies that aim to promote the inclusion of all members of a community, including those who are often marginalized or excluded. By using a participatory approach, promoting capacity building, ensuring accessible infrastructure, advocating for the rights of marginalized groups, promoting inclusive policies and programs, and fostering collaboration and partnerships, CBID can help to build more inclusive and equitable communities, contributing to sustainable development and economic growth.

Generating supportive conditions: community resources for the rehabilitation of disabled people

Creating enabling environments is an essential step towards mobilizing Local community resources for the rehabilitation of disabled people. An enabling environment refers to the physical, social, economic, and cultural conditions that facilitate the inclusion and participation of persons with disabilities in all aspects of community life. Here are some strategies for the same:

1. **Develop community-based rehabilitation programs:** Community-based rehabilitation (CBR) programs aim to provide rehabilitation services to persons with disabilities in their communities. CBR programs involve the active participation of community members and utilize local resources to promote the inclusion and participation of persons with disabilities.

2. **Sensitization and awareness-raising:** Sensitization and awareness-raising campaigns are important for mobilizing local community resources towards the rehabilitation of persons with disabilities. These campaigns can involve community education programs, outreach activities, and social marketing campaigns that aim to reduce stigma and discrimination towards persons with disabilities.

3. **Capacity building:** Capacity building is essential for mobilizing local community resources towards the rehabilitation of persons with disabilities. Capacity building programs can include training and education programs that aim to develop the skills and knowledge of community members in providing rehabilitation services to persons with disabilities.

4. **Partnership and collaboration:** Partnership and collaboration are essential for mobilizing local community resources towards the rehabilitation of persons with disabilities. Partnerships can involve working with local organizations, government agencies, and other stakeholders to develop inclusive policies and programs that promote the inclusion and participation of persons with disabilities.

5. **Accessible infrastructure:** Accessible infrastructure is important for creating enabling environments for persons with disabilities. This can include making public spaces, buildings, and transportation accessible, as well as providing accessible information and communication technologies.

6. **Economic empowerment:** Economic empowerment is an important strategy for mobilizing local community resources towards the rehabilitation of persons with disabilities. Economic empowerment programs can include vocational training and employment programs that aim to promote the economic independence of persons with disabilities.

In conclusion, creating enabling environments is essential for mobilizing local community resources towards the rehabilitation of persons with disabilities. Strategies for creating enabling environments can include developing community-based rehabilitation programs, sensitization and awareness-raising, capacity building, partnership and collaboration, accessible infrastructure, and economic empowerment. By mobilizing local community resources towards the rehabilitation of persons with disabilities, we can promote the inclusion and participation of persons with disabilities in all aspects of community life, contributing to sustainable development and economic growth.

Issues and challenges in rehabilitation of child with disability in the community

The rehabilitation of a child with a disability in the community can be challenging and requires the concerted effort of all stakeholders involved in the process. Some of the issues and challenges that may be encountered include:

1. **Limited access to rehabilitation services:** In many communities, access to rehabilitation services may be limited or non-existent. This could be due to a lack of qualified healthcare professionals, inadequate infrastructure, or inadequate funding. Without access to these services, children with disabilities may not receive the care and support they need to reach their full potential.

2. **Stigmatization and discrimination:** Children with disabilities may face stigma and discrimination within their communities. This can lead to social isolation, exclusion, and limited opportunities for education, employment, and social interaction. It can also affect their self-esteem and confidence, making it difficult for them to thrive.

3. **Inadequate education and training:** Healthcare professionals, caregivers, and family members may lack the necessary education and training to provide appropriate care and support to children with disabilities. This can lead to suboptimal care, delayed development, and increased dependence on others.

4. **Financial constraints:** The cost of rehabilitation services and equipment can be prohibitive, particularly for families with limited financial resources. This can limit access to care and lead to suboptimal outcomes for children with disabilities.

5. **Inadequate infrastructure:** In many communities, infrastructure may be inadequate to support the needs of children with disabilities. This can include lack of accessible transportation, buildings, and public spaces.

Without adequate infrastructure, children with disabilities may be unable to access important services and participate fully in their communities.

6. **Lack of community engagement and participation:** Rehabilitation efforts may be hampered by a lack of community engagement and participation. Without buy-in from the community, rehabilitation efforts may not be sustained over the long-term, limiting the impact on the lives of children with disabilities.

In order to overcome these challenges, it is important to take a comprehensive approach that involves all stakeholders, including healthcare professionals, caregivers, family members, and community members. This may involve improving access to rehabilitation services, addressing stigma and discrimination, providing education and training, developing affordable financing options, improving infrastructure, and engaging with the community to build support and sustainability. By addressing these challenges, we can help children with disabilities to reach their full potential and thrive in their communities.

CHAPTER FIVE

Role of community in education of children with disabilities

Community awareness about disabilities is essential for early identification, intervention, and education. By increasing awareness, we can reduce stigma and discrimination, promote inclusion, and ensure that children with disabilities receive the support and care they need to thrive. Some key strategies for improving community awareness include:

1. **Education campaigns:** Public education campaigns can help raise awareness about disabilities, including the signs and symptoms of various conditions and the importance of early identification and intervention. These campaigns can be targeted at parents, teachers, healthcare professionals, and the general public.
2. **Community events:** Hosting community events such as disability awareness days, fairs, and workshops can help promote understanding and acceptance of disabilities. These events can also provide opportunities for families of children with disabilities to connect and share their experiences.
3. **Inclusion in education:** Educating students about disabilities as part of the regular curriculum can help promote acceptance and understanding. In addition, including children with disabilities in mainstream education can help break down barriers and promote inclusion.
4. **Training for healthcare providers:** Healthcare professionals play an important role in identifying and treating disabled children. By providing training on early identification and intervention, healthcare

professionals can help ensure that children with disabilities receive the care they need as early as possible.

5. **Collaboration with community organizations:** Collaboration with community organizations that serve children with disabilities, such as advocacy groups and support groups, can help promote awareness and understanding. These organizations can also provide valuable resources and support to families of children with disabilities.

By improving community awareness about disabilities, we can help ensure that children with disabilities receive the care and support they need to reach their full potential. Early identification and intervention can make a significant difference in the lives of these children, and education can help promote acceptance and inclusion in the community.

Community support for home-based education in times of disasters

Community support is critical for home-based education and in times of disaster. Home-based education refers to the process of educating children in the home environment, rather than in a traditional school setting. This approach can be used for a variety of reasons, including health concerns, geographic isolation, and preference for alternative forms of education. In times of disasters, such as natural disasters or pandemics, home-based education can become necessary to ensure that children continue to receive an education when schools are closed or inaccessible. In this essay, we will discuss the importance of community support for home-based education and in times of disasters, as well as strategies for building and sustaining that support.

Home-based education:

Home-based education can offer many benefits to children, including more personalized instruction, flexibility in scheduling, and greater parental involvement in the learning process. However, it can also present challenges, particularly for families who lack the necessary resources and support. In order to succeed, families may need access to educational resources, such as textbooks and online learning tools, as well as support from their community.

Community support for home-based education can take many forms. For example, community organizations may provide resources and support to families, such as free textbooks or online learning tools. Local libraries can serve as a valuable resource for families, providing access to books, videos, and other educational materials. Community centers can also offer space for children to meet and collaborate on projects.

Another important form of community support for home-based education is mentorship. Mentors can provide guidance and support to families who are new to home-based education, sharing best practices and helping families navigate the challenges that may arise. Mentors can also provide social support to children, offering a sense of connection and belonging that may be lacking in the home environment.

Finally, community support for home-based education can take the form of advocacy. Community members can advocate for policies and programs that support home-based education, such as funding for online learning tools or support for families who are new to home-based education. By advocating for these policies and programs, community members can help ensure that all families have access to the resources and support they need to succeed.

In times of disasters:

In times of disasters, such as natural disasters or pandemics, schools may be closed or inaccessible, making home-based education necessary to ensure that children continue to receive an education. In these situations, community support for home-based education becomes even more critical.

One important form of community support in times of disaster is emergency preparedness. Communities can develop emergency plans that include provisions for home-based education, such as the provision of online learning tools or the establishment of mentorship programs for families who are new to home-based education. By including home-based education in emergency plans, communities can help ensure that children continue to receive an education even in the midst of a disaster.

Another important form of community support in times of disaster is collaboration. Community members can work together to develop and share educational resources, such as lesson plans and online learning tools, that can be used by families who are unable to access traditional schooling. Collaboration can also involve sharing of best practices and strategies for home-based education, as well as providing emotional support to families who may be experiencing stress and anxiety due to the disaster.

Finally, community support in times of disaster can take the form of advocacy. Community members can advocate for policies and programs that support home-based education during times of disasters, such as funding for online learning tools or support for families who are new to home-based education. By advocating for these policies and programs, community members can help ensure that all children have access to an education, even in the midst of a disaster.

Aganwadis and other governmental organizations to educate children with impairments

Aganwadis are government-run centers in India that provide early childhood education, nutrition, and healthcare to children under the age of six. These centers play a critical role in the education and development of young children, including those with disabilities. In this essay, we will discuss the importance of collaboration with Aganwadis and other governmental agencies for the education of children with disabilities, as well as strategies for building and sustaining that collaboration.

Importance of collaboration:

Collaboration with Aganwadis and other governmental agencies is important for several reasons. First, these agencies have the mandate to provide education and healthcare services to all children, including those with disabilities. By collaborating with these agencies, educators and healthcare professionals can ensure that children with disabilities receive the support and care they need to succeed.

Second, collaboration with Aganwadis and other governmental agencies can help ensure that children with disabilities receive early identification and intervention. Early identification and intervention are critical for children with disabilities, as they can help prevent or reduce the impact of disabilities on a child's development. By working together, educators and healthcare professionals can ensure that children with disabilities are identified early and receive appropriate interventions.

Third, collaboration with Aganwadis and other governmental agencies can help promote inclusion and reduce the stigma surrounding disabilities. By working together to provide education and healthcare services to all children, regardless of their abilities, we can promote a culture of inclusion and acceptance. This can help reduce the stigma and discrimination that children with disabilities may face in the community.

Strategies for collaboration:

There are several strategies that can be used to build and sustain collaboration with Aganwadis and other governmental agencies for the education of children with disabilities. These strategies include:

1. **Building relationships:** Building relationships with staff at Aganwadis and other governmental agencies is key to effective collaboration.

Educators and healthcare professionals should reach out to these agencies and establish regular communication channels to share information and resources.

2. **Providing training:** Providing training to staff at Aganwadis and other governmental agencies can help ensure that they have the knowledge and skills they need to identify and support children with disabilities. This training can include information on early identification and intervention, as well as strategies for promoting inclusion.

3. **Sharing resources:** Sharing resources, such as educational materials and assistive technology, can help ensure that all children, including those with disabilities, have access to the resources they need to succeed. Educators and healthcare professionals should work with Aganwadis and other governmental agencies to identify and share resources that can support the education and development of children with disabilities.

4. **Collaborating on interventions:** Collaborating on interventions, such as therapy and rehabilitation services, can help ensure that children with disabilities receive the support they need to thrive. Educators and healthcare professionals should work with Aganwadis and other governmental agencies to develop interventions that are tailored to the unique needs of each child.

5. **Advocating for policies:** Advocating for policies that support the education and development of children with disabilities can help ensure that all children have access to the resources and support they need to succeed. Educators and healthcare professionals should work with Aganwadis and other governmental agencies to advocate for policies that promote inclusion, early identification, and appropriate interventions for children with disabilities.

Conclusion:

Collaboration with Aganwadis and other governmental agencies is essential for the education and development of children with disabilities. By building relationships, providing training, sharing resources, collaborating on interventions, and advocating for policies, educators and healthcare professionals can ensure that children with disabilities receive the support and care they need to thrive. This collaboration can help promote inclusion, reduce stigma, and ensure that all

Community as a stakeholder in special and inclusive education

The community is an essential stakeholder in special and inclusive education. The community includes families, neighbors, businesses, organizations, and local government officials, among others. All of these stakeholders have a role to play in supporting the education and development of children with disabilities. In this essay, we will discuss the importance of community involvement in special and inclusive education, as well as strategies for building and sustaining that involvement.

Importance of community involvement:

Community involvement is critical for several reasons. First, the community can provide valuable support to families of children with disabilities. Families of children with disabilities may face unique challenges, such as social isolation and financial difficulties. By involving the community, families can receive emotional and practical support that can help them navigate these challenges.

Second, the community can help promote inclusion and reduce the stigma surrounding disabilities. By involving the community in special and inclusive education, we can raise awareness and promote understanding of the unique needs and abilities of children with disabilities. This can help reduce the stigma and discrimination that children with disabilities may face in the community.

Third, the community can provide resources and support to schools and educators. Schools and educators may lack the resources and expertise needed to support the education and development of children with disabilities. By involving the community, schools, and educators can access a range of resources and expertise that can help them meet the needs of all students, including those with disabilities.

Strategies for community involvement:

There are several strategies that can be used to build and sustain community involvement in special and inclusive education. These strategies include:

1. **Engaging families:** Engaging families of children with disabilities is essential for building community involvement. Schools and educators should reach out to families and involve them in decision-making processes, such as Individualized Education Program (IEP) meetings. This can help ensure that families are informed and empowered to advocate for their children's needs.

2. **Partnering with community organizations:** Partnering with community organizations, such as disability advocacy groups and non-profit organizations, can help schools and educators access resources and expertise. These organizations can also provide outreach and education to the community about the unique needs and abilities of children with disabilities.

3. **Involving local businesses:** Involving local businesses in special and inclusive education can provide valuable resources and support. For example, businesses can provide internships and job opportunities for students with disabilities, as well as donate funds and supplies to schools and programs.

4. **Working with local government officials:** Working with local government officials can help promote policies and initiatives that support special and inclusive education. Schools and educators can work with local officials to advocate for policies that promote inclusion, early identification, and appropriate interventions for children with disabilities.

5. **Promoting community events and activities:** Promoting community events and activities that celebrate the abilities of children with disabilities can help promote inclusion and reduce stigma. Schools and educators can organize events, such as disability awareness days, talent shows, and sports tournaments, that involve and showcase the abilities of children with disabilities.

Conclusion:

Community involvement is essential for the success of special and inclusive education. By engaging families, partnering with community organizations, involving local businesses, working with local government officials, and promoting community events and activities, we can build and sustain community involvement in special and inclusive education. This involvement can help provide support to families, promote inclusion and reduce stigma, and provide resources and support to schools and educators. Ultimately, this collaboration can help ensure that all students, regardless of their abilities, have access to the education and support they need to succeed.

Safeguarding children with disabilities and their families in the communities

Safeguarding children with disabilities and their families in the community is an essential aspect of ensuring that they are protected from harm, abuse, and neglect. Children with disabilities are more vulnerable to abuse and neglect due to their increased dependency on others for care and support. Therefore, it is crucial to implement measures that can safeguard these children and their families in the community. In this essay, we will discuss the issues related to safeguarding children with disabilities and their families in the community, as well as strategies to address them.

Issues related to safeguarding children with disabilities and their families:

1. **Limited access to resources:** Families of children with disabilities may have limited access to resources, such as health care, education, and financial support. This can lead to increased vulnerability to abuse and neglect.
2. **Stigmatization and discrimination:** Children with disabilities and their families may face stigmatization and discrimination in the community. This can make it difficult for them to access resources and support, and also increase their vulnerability to abuse and neglect.
3. **Lack of awareness and knowledge:** The community may lack awareness and knowledge about disabilities, which can lead to misunderstanding and mistreatment of children with disabilities and their families. This can increase the risk of abuse and neglect.

Strategies to safeguard children with disabilities and their families:

1. **Strengthening community networks:** Community networks, such as parent support groups, disability advocacy organizations, and local service providers, can provide support and resources to families of children with disabilities. By strengthening these networks, families can access the resources and support they need to protect their children.
2. **Promoting awareness and education:** Promoting awareness and education about disabilities can help reduce stigma and discrimination. This can be done through community events, workshops, and public education campaigns.
3. **Ensuring access to resources:** Ensuring that families of children with disabilities have access to essential resources, such as health care, education, and financial support, can help reduce their vulnerability to

abuse and neglect. This can be achieved by working with local service providers, government agencies, and non-profit organizations.

4. **Empowering families:** Empowering families of children with disabilities can help them become advocates for their children's rights and protection. This can be done by providing them with information, resources, and support to help them navigate systems and advocate for their children's needs.

5. **Implementing policies and procedures:** Implementing policies and procedures that protect children with disabilities from harm, abuse, and neglect can help safeguard them in the community. This can include developing protocols for reporting and investigating suspected abuse and neglect, as well as training community members on how to recognize and respond to these situations.

Conclusion:

Safeguarding children with disabilities and their families in the community is essential for their protection and well-being. By strengthening community networks, promoting awareness and education, ensuring access to resources, empowering families, and implementing policies and procedures, we can address the issues related to safeguarding children with disabilities and their families in the community. These strategies can help reduce the vulnerability of children with disabilities to abuse and neglect, and ensure that they have access to the resources and support they need to thrive in the community.